MW01223042

leaf shakings

North Hills Monthly Magazine 2016

Villa Vuoto Publications
Copyright © 2016

ISBN: 1 539942 79 1
EAN-13: 978 1 539942 79 5
First Edition
615

Text and illustrations by
Matthew Schlueb

June 21, 2016

Hi Matthew,

As always, this is beautifully written.

I do have a concern, however, that in the last couple of columns, you seem to be getting further and further away from the topic of architectural issues for homeowners. While I love your writing, I'm not sure that we're delivering on what the series has promised to readers.

In your next column, could you perhaps focus more on the architectural aspect of things, such as you did with your column on designing a home to fit naturally into the space where it's being built, or the importance of certain rooms in the house? While I do not want to limit your creativity, I'd like the column to be more centered on the architectural aspect of things.

Please let me know if you'd like to discuss. Thanks!

Vanessa

Vanessa Orr
Executive Editor
North Hills Monthly Magazine

Who Speaks for the Trees?

I always find this a curious time, the first week of a new year, marked by pine trees slumped over the curb. Just a week ago, those trees were center stage - brought into our homes, decorated with lights and gifts laid at their feet. Now alongside recycling bins, soon to become mulch for flower beds this Spring.

What is this strange relationship we have with trees? Why have our customs and traditions become so wrapped up in them? It seems a backyard is not complete without a treehouse for the kids. And yet, it is often the parents that derive the most pleasure from them, daydreams of more youthful days.

Front yards landscaped with ornamental cherries blossoming to mark the start of summer, maples bursting in shades of yellow and red at summer's end. It is no surprise neighborhoods filled with trees hold higher re-sale values than those without.

Which makes me wonder, why do developers spend time and money clearing lots of trees, only to re-plant new ones after homes are built? A homebuyer must wait years for the day when these young trees will mature, once again spreading canopies of shade reminiscent of the older trees long gone.

I can only imagine it is a matter of convenience - a clear, flat lot is far easier to drop a house onto, than siting a house amongst trees, accounting for roots, falling branches, veiled sunlight. In the eyes of a builder, trees are obstacles. So little consideration for these assets offering value to a property.

Last Fall I was disheartened by one such builder on a lot I had considered speculating myself. It was filled with giant oaks and white pines that had another century or two of growth still in them. Two acres of awe inspiring heights, each one trying to outdo the next, reaching for the sky.

I had visions of a house nestled and protected by such sentries, echoing the songs of birds throughout the year. But, it was not to be. Instead, they were felled, every last one, site cleared to the very edges. The lot became a barren patch surrounded by wooded properties on all sides, an open wound crying out for cover.

Root balls pulled out, branches stripped off, trunks piled up as pick-up-sticks waiting to be loaded and carted off to the mills. Such is the beginnings of the wood floors and cabinets in the homes we build. It calls to mind a story I read as a child, of a tree giving everything it had for the needs of a growing boy.

Aside from the many offerings the tree made, it always struck me as one sided. There must be a better way of doing things. But, I am reminded of a comment made once by a friend, "these proud trees, appreciated and brought to a full potential by our use, worthy of their mighty size and strength."

Maybe this is as it should be. Trees cleansing air to breathe, then cooling it with shading leaves, finally harvested for wood to build. Yet, this may be over-simplified. Home to birds' nests, burrowing squirrels, clinging lichen, tunneling larvae, trees are a microcosm of life far beyond our narrow human demands.

The lungs of the earth, their tips stitching together a bridge between clouds overhead and earth under our feet. These trees can be handled in a smarter way, a more fitting and respectful relationship. There was a time when builders knew trees by characteristics unique to each species, strengths and weaknesses to build from.

Evergreens on the northwest side of a house, to shield cold winter winds. Deciduous trees to the south for shading summer heat, then allowing warm sunlight through when needed, after the leaves have fallen. With a little thoughtful consideration, a house can be constructed that fits to the landscape, not the other way around.

And in the long run, isn't this best? If our communities are to last, we will need to consider the things around us, the things we use to make our homes. If we do no more than exploit, we will soon find our lands desolate, just as so many legendary forests have gone by civilizations of the past.

Where today are the Sycamore stands that once lined the waterways of America? Where are the Oaks of Europe, the Cyprus of Asia, the Acacia of Africa? They have vanished as snow before a summer sun.

The lifespan of a tree is measured in centuries, but can be taken in a day. Such acts take years to undo. How can a storied life be ended with so little concern? Are we so distracted we no longer notice what is missing?

With a new year upon us, consider preserving the trees that enrich your home. If you find yourself looking for a new home, take a closer look at the trees standing on the properties you consider. Your home will be the better for noticing, as you become more attuned to what the trees have to say.

Dec 30, 2015 09:31AM, Published by North Hills Monthly Magazine, Categories: Home+Garden
http://www.northhillsmonthly.com/2015/12/30/97922/who-speaks-for-the-trees

605

Holzwege

"Look!" Standing frozen in the woods outside our house, Olin called with a hush. We were climbing a gentle slope and just above us a buck was wondering by, picking at the underbrush.

"Keep quiet", I whispered to my other son, Oskar, who was walking next to me. All three of us became statues, as the lone deer continued along a well worn path.

Then suddenly he took note of us. Not sure if he could see us, most likely smelled us, since there was a slight breeze from below. He continued looking in our direction, curious and slowly working closer, stomping a rear leg, shaking his head, trying to get us to flinch.

We waited patiently, quiet and still. Eventually he got within twenty feet of Olin, who was another twenty feet out front of us. Moving my hands like a sloth, I eased the phone out of my pocket and snapped a picture of the two of them checking each other out. Then, he decided to get back to feeding, turned up hill and went on his way.

Olin was excited the rest of the day, a brief exchange with nature on our morning walk was enough to send his mind racing. "Why do deers always walk on the same trampled down path?" he asked, "...to keep from getting lost?"

I replied, "Our house sits off a busy road that was once an Indian trail." - the Kuskusky Path, a pre-colonial pass between two Lenape Indian settlements, what became Allegheny City on the Northside and present day New Castle further north. "Well, ancient Indian trails often came from deer paths, the natives would follow while hunting them."

"And, deer follow water runoffs to find streams for drinking." I continued, "Rainwater gathers like veins, cutting through the soil, down the path of least resistance. These channels erode away vegetation, defining seams between thickets." Holzwege, they called them - naturally forming wood ways, meandering meridians that wildlife navigate easily.

"As it turns out, those natural paths follow patterns deep underground. Soft sediment fissures that fill between rock formations, become depressions forming variations in the landscape." These materials have been disintegrated by temperatures, ground down by glaciers, eroded by wind and water, sculpted by tireless forces qualifying each other. They are all externally modified by time as they modify this earth in a ceaseless procession of change.

"In the end, the major roads we travel today, trace the earlier Indian trails, who followed deer paths, which were following rainwater gathering toward a stream, formed by soft spots in the soil fingering between rock formations deep within the earth." It seems after all, these routes we take are not by chance. They are founded on repeated journeys, trusted wisdom that follows those who come before us.

Last week I was called to the South Hills, by a homeowner that just moved into a house they built and was unable to sleep at night, due to loud trucks driving up a nearby route. There was also a train track within earshot and a flight path overhead. This house seemed to be at the crossroads of every mode of transportation and the homeowner was looking to me to solve the noise problem.

I walked around the outside of the house, measuring decibel levels with a sound meter app on my phone, noting the noise level drops from retaining walls blocking the line of sight to the busy road down the hillside. It snaked through rock outcroppings on both sides, which amplified the traffic noise up the valley, directly inline to their backyard.

I then took readings inside the house, going from room to room, registering the increases caused by vaulted ceilings, wood floors, and large expanse of windows. Unfortunately, as I explained to them, the best solution was things to be done before the house was finished. Such as selecting windows with a high Sound Transmission Class (STC) rating and using a spray foam insulation in the walls and ceiling to seal off air infiltration, as sound travels through the air leaks around openings in the house perimeter.

In addition to those measures, a double layer of 1/2" drywall held off the wall studs with resilient channels on the inside, along with a stone or brick veneer on the outside is one of the most effect sound barriers in a residential setting. But, this news was a little too late for this household. Wanting to avoid a major retrofit, involving time, money and quite a bit of dust in a recently completed house, their simplest course of action was to move.

As an architect, I am hired to avoid such pitfalls. When selecting a piece of property on which to build a house, many factors come into play. For a family building a home for the first time, some of these factors are overlooked. If a house is designed well, the site will determine its features and character. Unfortunately, with builders who use stock plans, often the house design is not adjusted for the site. And in this case, a builder with an architect on staff, adjustments still did not address the homeowner's concerns over the builder's.

I have found my most valued toolset is attuning to the surroundings, keeping my senses sharp to take notice of these subtle cues in the landscape which have great influence on the life around us. I go into the circumstances and come out with a design from within. Much as the deer and natives follow the landscape. There are good reasons things take the course they do. And over the years, I have made far fewer mistakes following that flow, rather than ignoring it.

Jan 29, 2016 05:24PM, Published by North Hills Monthly Magazine, Categories: Home+Garden
http://www.northhillsmonthly.com/2016/01/29/101177/not-all-landscapes-are-equal

Roots of a Home

When I was a kid, we lived in a neighborhood with front lawns the size of postage stamps. Just big enough to lay in the grass and daydream up in the clouds. Spring was the best time for that, as cotton balls churned and swept by. Now I live in the woods, so my kids lay on a bed of leaves, looking up at tree canopies filling the sky.

"Our trees are so slender and tall, why don't we have any good ones for climbing?" my youngest son Olin asked on one such afternoon slumbering outdoors.

"They are racing to the sun, each one trying to outgrow the next, competing for sunlight at the top." my other son Oskar replied.

"It's true, they need sunlight, but trees are more cooperative than competitive." I said, "In our woods, many of the trees are related and all of them are networked together by their roots underground. Trees have found it more efficient to share sunlight, air and rain. Each tree lives longer by being a part of the group, with a reciprocal relationship exchanging nutrients when in need from those with more than enough."

"When a new sprout takes root," I elaborated, "they are so far down here on the forest floor, what little sunlight makes it through become dancing spots from a spring breeze tickling tree leaves. As a result, the older trees of the forest nurse these young saplings, giving them the sugars they can't photosynthesize themselves."

"We might not have branches for climbing, but we can interact with our trees in more amazing ways." I told Olin. "Every step into the woods has miles of microscopic roots tangled together underfoot, much like the network of neurons in our brains. When we notice a new tree, our mental map of the forest changes in our heads, new connections are made to physically model our perception of that tree."

"In the same way," I continued, "the tree responds to us walking through the woods. Roots in the top soil compress, carbon dioxide we exhale is absorbed, our shadow cast is felt by their trunk receptive to light. These things are subtle, many people don't even notice. But, they are there happening nonetheless - traces of us can be found in the tree, just as remnants of the tree are in our head stored as a memory."

When we built our house a decade ago, I wanted to set it in the woods, so we could look out from our bedroom windows at the birds nesting high up in the treetops. To do so required cutting a few down. I tried to find a clearing, but none fit a house. My neighbor with similar intent, cut down all the trees within falling distance of his house - to avoid possible damage from violent storms. I wasn't so cautious, only the ones within the house footprint came out.

But everyone is different, just as no two trees are alike. What feels like a safe distance for one can feel too distant to another. I studied these proximity relationships with my graduate thesis in architecture. I learned how things move about, reacting to each other, finding balance points where everything feels most comfortable. It happens at every scale, from insects living under leaves, to the planets hurling across the night sky.

Much of my studies examined formal aspects of weight and space, manipulating awareness, making refinements to identify perceptual thresholds. However, living in the woods I have come to realize the significance of things more nuanced, less visual. Our individual personalities have far more to say in the matter.

A daydreamer can walk through the woods unaware of things going on around them. While a child afraid of the dark, walking through just after sunset will hear the snap of a twig or rustling leaves. The forest is not singular or static, it is defined by our perceptions.

And our perceptions are based primarily on scale. We give very little credence to the things beyond the range of our senses. Forests are often thought of as peaceful places, but there is quite a bit of chatter going on between the trees, swapping signals underground and on the wind. Our perception is narrowed, to the things that concern us. What need do we have for the things trees are saying?

When designing a house, I have found it essential to take these individualized perceptions into consideration. Sunlight casting across a kitchen island, warming a granite surface, may start the morning off right for some, just as a cup of coffee will for another. The table a parent reaches across to set is not the same table to the toddler crawling underneath. To layout a kitchen, and all the other rooms of a house, the perspective of each family member is vital. Taking care of these multiple viewpoints in a household, not only creates a more meaningful house, but more importantly, gets to the root of the network that defines a home.

Feb 26, 2016 05:37PM, Published by North Hills Monthly Magazine, Categories: Home+Garden, Today
http://www.northhillsmonthly.com/2016/02/26/103631/roots-of-a-home

Cherry Blossoms

Not long ago, I was invited into the home of a Quaker woman. We sat in her kitchen filled with colorful memories, as a winters afternoon sunlight filtered in across a well worn table. She had tutored a young Iraqi woman in English, who had immigrated with her husband. They had a daughter and a second on the way. The woman's heart had grown close to this family, and the two bedroom house, one more than needed, had planted a seed in her mind.

As we sat at this painted wood table, its surface a witness to a lifetime of home making, she explained to me how she wanted to add on a mother-in-law suite to her home, one she could move into so that this Iraqi family could have her existing house. As she said, "My happiest times are when I have people sitting around the fire circle, talking, laughing, singing into a night sky. Why not create a home to have more experiences like that?"

So, we met a few more times at this table, reviewing drawings, discussing plans to build such an addition. The table's four legs defined a space we shared in those meetings, just as four tall trees stood sentry outdoors at the corners of her home, defining a space for this new suite to be placed. The original house was a gabled box, painted blue siding, with an entry in an oddly placed side door. We decided to create a new entry, a connector between her new suite, modeled in character but scaled slightly smaller, and the original house now paired.

In the spring construction began, as her excitement spilled over into endless smiles each time I saw her. Walls were painted, wood floors laid, cabinetry placed. It wasn't long before her new family moved in, their first night on Thanksgiving Day. I imagine the fire that night was memorable for all of them, a new family made from two homes of distant cultures, now close in proximity of space and hearts.

I returned the following year, after some time settled in. The kitchen table was still there, in the same spot snugged against that window facing a setting sun. However, now the top was masked by a printed cloth trimmed with embroidery. Much of her original furnishings remained, handed down along with the house, for another lifetime of use. But the space had changed, a new layer was added to the stories these things told, rendering something different, something special.

In such instances we see the full significance of the flower sacrifice.
Perhaps the flowers appreciate the full significance of it.
They are not cowards, like men. Some flowers glory in death -
certainly the Japanese cherry blossoms do, as they freely surrender
themselves to the winds.
Anyone who has stood before the fragrant avalanche at Yoshino must
realize this. For a moment they hover like bejeweled clouds and dance;
then, as they sail away on laughing waters, they seem to say:
Farewell, O Spring! We are on to Eternity.

If an architect is lucky, just such a flower blossom drifts by, offering a rare gift into the true measure of a home. It is not the timbers felled, squared and plumbed to support a roof overhead. It is not the room they define, decorated with finger paintings, tablecloths, and flowerpots. Nor is it the people living inside, sheltered, warmed, sharing their time together. It is the mixture of all these things, a blending that makes a home.

An aged painted table, edges eased by endless caresses, hands in conversation, communal meals, moments shared. An aged tree canopy, limbs lowered sheltering shade, protective of this woman reading stories to a granddaughter, making a happy place.

March 31, 2016 10:23AM, Published by North Hills Monthly Magazine, Categories: Home+Garden, Today
http://www.northhillsmonthly.com/2016/03/31/106613/cherry-blossoms

Treehouses

One of my favorite summers as a child, was spent building a treehouse in our backyard. My friends and I needed a place for our secret club to meet and elevation in a tree, where our little sisters would not follow, made the perfect spot. All kinds of details were added, ropes on pulleys to hull up treasures, false floors with removable boards for hiding code books, and a mounted telescope to keep a lookout for spying sisters.

I remember conversations my Dad had with neighbors inquiring about this tree he planted in our backyard. He selected an Eastern Sycamore because it was fast growing, to quickly mature and provide a canopy of shade over our backyard patio. Fortunately for me, I was growing up along with it, so its lowest branches were just the right height to encourage climbing.

Although sycamores of the Ohio valley are some of the most massive trees in North America, the most beautiful sycamores I have found are in Southern California. Conditions there are ideal for spreading out long, low, twisting and turning branches. The kind of branches that make anyone with a childhood of tree climbing excited by the potential. I imagine this is what my father had envisioned when he was instructed to cut off the top of our tree when it was just a sapling – to discourage tall growth, so branches would spread out over our backyard.

However, our tree was not so easily persuaded, it clearly had other intentions. That fateful trimming was only a minor delay. The canopy did not fill out horizontally, as my father had hoped. The following summer, the trunk sprouted out to the side of the stunted top, then turning upward as it continued on it way reaching for the sky above the roofline of our house.

All the better for me, higher heights to climb, to see things from a bird's perspective. During my prime climbing years as a child, that bend in the trunk had grown to the height of my second floor bedroom window, which overlooked the tree. The highest point I would dare climb. But when I did, I was rewarded by this truncated turn, just the right shape for reclining back to get a close-up view of clouds overhead.

It is these turns in a trunk that become the physical record, placeholders of memories, markings of past acts in the life of a tree. A woodworker friend of mine celebrates these variations that reveal a history, allow the tree to speak through the material he works with in creating tables, chairs, doors. Each palimpsest gives pause, stirring curiosity and wonder about what might have occurred one day years ago. What course was set by a father pruning the top of a sapling? Now recorded in this strange canopy, clearly not the result of a natural occurrence.

If our backyard tree is cut down someday, maybe by a future homeowner seeking more sunlight, it may be processed into boards. A second life, as my woodworker friend calls it, to be made into useful things for a home. As an architect, I seek out unusual materials, those with unique grain telling a story of a hard, worn life of growing. So much time goes into the making of materials, some more than others. Trees can take centuries to age, while the veins in a slab of marble, by contrast, take millions of years.

Recently, I had a homeowner quip "These things are not that important, it is all so materialistic." There is some truth to that statement – I have witnessed far too many designers wax poetic and spend far too much of their client's money on material finishes they believed were absolutely necessary. In my opinion, if the design of a space hinges on one particular material selection, the space itself has far greater problems to address.

However, there is also something to be said for the integrity of building materials. Architectural finishes do not need to be exotic, luxurious or precious to create a beautiful space. Even the most basic of materials can elevate the feel of a space, when treated in a simple, honest manner, reflecting their true nature. And in the end, don't these materials, such as wood that we take selfishly for our own use, deserve the respect and reverence of any living thing? Before wood is efflorescent patterns, silken textures or sinuous grains, it is first the life of a tree.

April 30, 2016 12:07PM, Published by North Hills Monthly Magazine, Categories: Home+Garden, Today
http://www.northhillsmonthly.com/2016/04/30/109181/history-of-building-materials-adds-to-appreciation

A Cabinet of Curiosities

Summer is the season for kids. Out from school, boundless energy unleashed on varieties of activity. My own sons look forward to spending long days wondering the woods in our backyard. Combing the creek for crayfish and hidden treasures. My oldest son Oskar, has filled the drawers in his bedroom with things he has found - intriguing and curious stones, bones, pine cones, walnuts, leaves, feathers, honeycombs, insects, egg shells, nests. The Carnegie Museum of Natural History owes him an honorary membership for his efforts.

"What are you saving these for?" his mother asks. The answer is old as human history. This collecting impulse formalized during the sixteenth century age of scientific discovery as the Kunstkammer or art chamber. A precursor to the museum, these dedicated rooms were a microcosm of the world, collections of curiosities symbolizing man's control over the wild outdoors, housed inside in an orderly fashion. A place to wonder, invoking curiosity of strange and interesting objects.

By the height of the Victorian era, the treatment of rooms in homes passed from the golden age of architecture to the gilded age of decoration. Architectural features which were part of the organism of every house became the superficial application of ornament totally independent of structure. Household ornaments were divided into three groups: bric-à-brac (odds and ends), bibelots (trinkets), and objet d'art (art).

Regardless of type, there is no shortage of spots to place these things in our homes today - fireplace mantels, bookshelves, end tables, curio cabinets dedicated solely to collectibles ...they seem inescapable. Clearly collecting is a human condition. But where does this instinct to collect come from?

In earlier times, when physical survival was more in the balance, gathering and storing up food for the winter was a way of life, entire traditions are based on it - Thanksgiving, Halloween, Octoberfest. I imagine that a fear of shortage plays quite a bit into the psyche of collecting.

But we now live in a time of global transportation enabling seasonal foods year-round and refrigeration in which to keep them. The instinct to hoard is no longer necessary, so it has mutated into something sentimental, a collection of things memorable becoming the ornaments of a home. Every home is defined by these objects. They speak to the memories and experiences of a homeowner. These objects we display in our homes preserve earlier moments in our lives, our younger selves we cling to, not ready to let go.

The houses we find ourselves occupying in planned communities, that appear repetitive, cookie-cutter on the outside, reveal an individuality and uniqueness on the inside by way of these personal mementos. The house is given two sides, an interior and exterior face, space becomes divided into public and private. The treasures we hold inside, our true home, are kept safe by this external chamber, revealed only to those we invite in.

Then along came the Modern movement, the invention of machine manufacturing and a drive toward standardization. The eclectic assortment of personalized nic-nacs decorating the home appeared cluttered, needing purged. Tout ce qui n'est pas nécessaire est nuisible - Everything that is not necessary is detrimental. The supreme excellence is simplicity.

However, something was lost by this streamlining. Our desire to collect did not go away. The more we cleared out the space of our home, the stronger the desire to fill it would consume us. Our consumer-based, market economy answered our calls. And today, we find our homes invaded by an Internet-Of-Things, one object at a time. A new collection of automated things, speaking to us in more ways than just reminiscing.

Where is all this heading? The future is not so easily foretold. But, one thing is for certain - as long as humans are in the picture, if we are to hold onto our humanity, these keepers of stories will continue to litter our homes. For if you don't have a good story to tell, what is the point of a drawer full of things?

May 31, 2016 01:43PM, Published by North Hills Monthly Magazine, Categories: Home+Garden, Today
http://www.northhillsmonthly.com/2016/05/31/112668/a-cabinet-of-curiosities

Fairy Gardens

From an airplane the earth is like a poached egg, a liquid spherical mass contained in a wrinkled skin. Saturated with water on the surface, constantly in the process of evaporating and condensing.

From an airplane you can see the clouds that nestle in a valley, burry a home or assure abundance of crops. Clouds no longer blow by, but become a network in symphony when viewed from the sky.

Just before sunrise, water vapor suspended in the realm of an airplane precipitates, covering the whole earth in dew. Then suddenly the sun bursts through the horizon's edge, the rays distance is enough for the whole day. Gnawing, churning the atmosphere, densities begin to operate, air masses gliding over each other.

From an airplane the shades of grass reveal the degree of humidity in the soil. The law of gradients above or under the ground, the earth is not a uniform green. Water as vapor, dew, eventually a gathering river on a rotating top spinning at an inclined plane is manipulated by this faraway star.

The view from an airplane is not rushed but slow, unbroken, the most precise one can wish. One can recognize the rooftop of a settler on a vast landscape, see the immensity of influence not often seen living each day so close to the surface. Perspective from above is quite different, transforming, meditative.

Such is the allure of a fairy garden. Our youngest son, Olin, along with his mother went to the Phipps' plant sale on Mother's Day and bought his first bonsai. A miniature conifer with dark green needles, yellowing at the tip, he trimmed it with a selection of fairy sized fauna, a park bench, and a magic urn for casting wishes.

Colored with patches of moss, spreading ground cover and dashes of fuchsia flowers, this garden in a pot holds his imagination as he mists it with water each day.

"Where is the fairy's house?" Surely there must be a house, he thought. So, we pulled out a block of clay to shape one by hand. Windows and doors were pressed in with small little fingertips. Then a chance wood firing with a potter friend and his fairy house was complete, scaled to tuck in under the canopy of his rabbit size pine.

How could such a giant of the forest be so tiny? What sorcery has been invoked to keep such a spirit caged to these proportions? The time and methods may be unknown, but their effects are unmistakable. These miniaturized plantings, stirring the minds of children, hold the same effect as an airplane flight overhead.

When our point of view is shifted, looking in on something from above, we comprehend the way things unfold, the interconnections of greater forces playing out in each life below. Fairy tales are more than a captivating story or lesson to be learned. They transform our thinking, to a mind's eye. An eye that sometimes catches a glimpse of a sprite as it flutters by.

Jun 30, 2016 08:56AM, Published by North Hills Monthly Magazine, Categories: Home+Garden, Today
http://www.northhillsmonthly.com/2016/06/30/115712/airplanes-and-fairy-gardens-seeing-things-from-a-different-perspective

Not All Decks Are Created Equal

If you are anything like me - the summer season starts off with a list of projects to do around the house before summer's end. A list that grows, more often than shortens. So, if this third month of summer enters with a deck project still in the planning stages - the following are a few things you might consider in selecting an exterior decking material.

There is no substitute for the romance and feel of a natural wood. Man-made composite decking options may be lower maintenance, however they have a synthetic look and feel, no soul in my opinion. And, if natural wood doesn't appeal enough to your sensitivities, unlike petroleum based composite materials, wood is completely renewable when sustainably grown and harvested - even with a carbon footprint that sequesters rather than contributes to climate change.

As far as maintenance goes, if hosed down at the end of each season on a bright sunny or windy day to dry quickly, wood will last for years. And, if you don't like a naturally weathered soft silvery grey appearance but prefer wood's virgin color tones, a water resistant, UV preservative stain applied every two or three years is all that is needed. Personally, I have found the satisfaction and relationship created by maintaining a deck over the years has been rewarding, the kind of thing gained by tending a garden.

If you are sold on a natural wood deck, it's important to understand that the material is in a state of continual change. So-called "rot" is really a beautiful and necessary step in a tree's contribution toward the larger web of life on our planet. Decomposition breaking down returns and replenishes the soil with a lifetime of nutrients collected during the photosynthesis process. As sunlight and wind dries out fallen wood, it will expand and split exposing entry points for water. This results in further swelling, supporting mold and fungi growth, which along with insects consume the fibers as a food source. When in contact with ground soils or climbing vines and other vegetation, the process accelerates. Our tendency as the owner of a wood deck, is slowing this natural process to appreciate its full beauty and integrity - do not be under the illusion this grand cycle can be altogether stopped.

The slower woods, the ones taking their time in this cycle of life (i.e. greatest "rot" resistance), not surprisingly are the more costly in our capitalistic marketplace. Black locust, Mexican teak, south Florida ipe, California redwood and bald cypress top this list. Other beneficial characteristics to look for in selecting wood are tight grain making the wood denser and heavier but stronger; the slower heartwood which is usually darker than the sapwood; and quarter sawn (vs. flat sawn) making it less likely to warp or cup. If only flat sawn is available, be sure to lay the boards with the crown (bark side) up to prevent water ponding.

Black locust is the most local of all the wood species, found growing in our Midwestern temperate region. Ranging from a pale greenish yellow to darker brown in color, darkening to a russet brown with age. Although grains are typically straight, this high density hardwood makes it difficult to nail or screw. However, this also makes it second only to hickory as the strongest and stiffest domestic timber, unsurpassed in stability. Best of all, it is one of the least threaten species with regards to deforestation, so with my clients, it is usually my first recommendation.

Mexican teak has high density and excellent stability, but low availability so it is best when needed in small quantities. Part of that low availability is a result of a slow growth technique on plantations, to mimic the soil and precipitation characteristics of the old growth tropical forests in Southeastern Asia, which resulted in teak's legendary grain pattern and golden brown color. Low availability and typically only in small pieces both contribute to one of the highest priced woods on the market.

South Florida ipe is a tropical hardwood, extremely hard and very high density with excellent stability, also with low availability. Its dark rich crimson color heats up to the touch in full sun. A smooth finish and tight grain results in no splinters, but heavy boards that are difficult to cut and drill. Therefore it is typically installed with hidden clips or biscuits. Does not take stains well, but accepts finish if weathered a couple months to leach out excess oils.

California redwood is a softwood with low density that easily damages from heavy foot traffic. Lightweight and stiff with good stability, it resisting warping, checking and splitting. Its open celled structure contains little or no pitch or resins, absorbing and retaining stains easily. However, it is the natural beauty of the light to rich dark red color that adds to its popularity and has resulted in its depletion down to only 1% of the old growth stands remaining in the Pacific Northwest.

Bald cypress is a softwood conifer native to the southeastern United States, thriving in flood lands and swamps. Light yellowish brown in color, sometimes with pockets of darker wood resulting from wetland fungi attacks. A medium density with good stability, it is widely available and therefore not a threatened species of extinction.

Western red cedar is a softwood with low density, good stability, but a tendency to splinter. Has a natural hardiness that changes its moisture content to closely match the atmosphere. Light brown to salmon pink in color, often with random streaks or bands of darker red brown areas. It is highly available, but avoid old growth as they are in danger of extinction. Has a moderate resistance to decay, with a mixed resistance to insect attacks.

European larch is a softwood conifer widely available, harvested as construction lumber with good stability. Natural resins offer a moderate resistance to decay, but have a tendency to gum up saw blades. Ranges from yellow to a medium reddish brown in color. Knots are common, but are usually small in size.

Southern yellow pine has the lowest natural resistance to decay, but when pressure treated exceeds all other natural woods. Low density and high strength make it the strongest of all softwoods, although it is susceptible to splits, twists and shrinkage. These facts combined with wide availability and low cost make it the most popular wood sold. Naturally golden yellow in color, its heartwood does not accept preservatives and therefore not decay resistant, appearing tan or pink instead of the green color of the treated sapwood. Because of the chemicals used to pressure treat, always use gloves and mask when handling and never burn it.

For more information on selecting the right wood for your summer projects, contact the Forest Stewardship Council (FSC), a non profit organization certifying lumber that is harvested in a legal and sustainable manner.

Jul 31, 2016 10:59PM, Published by North Hills Monthly Magazine, Categories: Home+Garden, Today
http://www.northhillsmonthly.com/2016/07/31/118280/not-all-decks-are-created-equal

Waldbäume

Living with a forest of trees on the slope of a valley in southwestern Pennsylvania, there is a certain time of day just before sunset, when the sun is hidden from view behind a western hill, but still casting sunlight on the trees to the east. The moment lasts only a few minutes, however it is the best light of day, the magic of the forest comes to life.

A slight breeze tickles a few trees high in their peak, sunlight dances from one branch to the next. Soaking bright green leaves in an amber glow that weaves through the depth of canopy in dimensional pockets of light and shadow.

Waldbäume, forest trees, are not the same as a solitary tree isolated by a well manicured lawn. This light of the forest reveals the fullness of trees, their true measure. As an architect, they remind me of the potential in light, to create a meaningfulness felt by a wonder of nature's endlessness.

Earlier this summer, my family traveled to Pompeii, visiting the ruins from an eruption of Mount Vesuvius nearly two thousand years ago. A roman city clad in stone, trees were confined to interior courts, not found along the streets. However, the stones that lined these streets, told another story of light, revealing a secret that has been hidden for some time.

Irregular shaped stones filled these streets and in between spaces at corner joints were filled in with coin sized fragments of Italian white marble. The Romans were resourceful people, nothing wasted. Not even moonlight, which reflected off these small pieces of stone, appearing to the eye as twinkling stars on full moon nights.

I am not sure we would notice such nuanced light today, certainly not when drowned out by a street light. Our electric world has an abundance of light, day and night. Sensitivities have dulled to the subtleties of light. We live in a time that is experiencing an easing of precision, by distancing ourselves from a tactile existence.

The typical suburban home illustrates this point - house and lot are created with as few shadows as possible, exposing interiors to a flood of light. Windows are not carefully placed, apertures metering light. Rather, they are lesions, growing across exterior walls, without intention. Eaves are more like a ripple of trimwork marking the transition from wall to roof, than an overhang to shade and provide cover from the sun.

Inside, walls and ceilings are painted white, dispelling shadows in the farthest corners. When music is amplified by a loudspeaker, the greater part of its charm is lost, so too beauty vanishes under the harsh glare of light. Brightness may provide good lighting for the tasks at hand in an operating room, but it is the quality of light on the theatrical stage, measured and balanced, that captures the dramatics of life.

We must be attentive to achieve such an effect. Curtains that filter light homogeneous, muted without soul, must be pulled back to establish a connection to the outdoors unfiltered. For a home to feel as if it was made for us, openings must be proportioned to the scale of a human being. It is the relationship of our body to the space, defined by a window fitted as a suit, when just the right amount of sunlight pouring in will resonate with our soul.

We are creatures of light, emotionally and physically. And, our houses should celebrate this. Fluctuations of intensity in rhythmic waves as clouds drift past, remind us that sunlight is a living, breathing thing - not the stagnant illumination from artificial lighting.

Daily acts are more pleasing when experienced within the variations of natural light, communing with the sun. Furnishings placed to receive sunlight cast across their surface, shadows articulating form. When a room is composed as a whole, daylighting timed with ritual acts - morning coffee, an afternoon snack - a meaningfulness returns.

In the design of a house, nothing is more important than light. Without it, a house is only good for sleeping. An architect knows it is the crafting of light, its modulations carving out of space, that makes for a home. And maybe by handling sunlight with a little more care, our eyes may soon appreciate the delicacy of moonlight and the stars overhead.

Aug 31, 2016 10:31AM, Published by North Hills Monthly Magazine, Categories: Travel, Today
http://www.northhillsmonthly.com/2016/08/31/120933/how-much-light-is-enough-

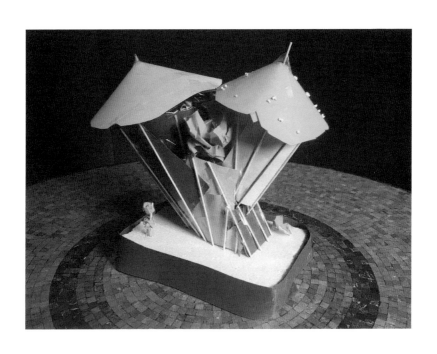

613

The Spiraling Housing Market

You may have noticed, the thunderhead clouds this summer seem bigger than they have been in past years. Much taller and robust, stretching across the entire sky. Not sure if it is greater concentrations of moisture in the atmosphere or larger currents stirring up the air, but the forecasters are predicting a more active hurricane season than usual.

That is a good thing for us in the home building business, because it extends the construction season later in the year. Traditionally, concrete is not poured past Thanksgiving. However, in the years I have been practicing architecture in this region, heavy hurricane seasons in the Caribbean translate into clear skies over Pittsburgh. Hurricanes seem to gather up all of our clouds, pulling them into concentrated spirals down south.

As a result, builders rush to squeeze in housing starts that would normally be left until next Spring. A house framed up and enclosed before the first snow falls, provides steady indoor work through the winter, to be finished and made ready for an early summer move in. Such is the pattern of the suburban housing market in southwestern Pennsylvania.

In the city however, housing is very different in many ways. A friend of mine makes a living off flipping houses in Lawrenceville, one of the nation's hottest real estate markets in recent years. He renovates townhouses from last century, putting in new heating, plumbing, electric, replacing cabinets, flooring, a fresh coat of paint. With an eye for the hipster marketplace, a contemporary looking interior can turn a good profit.

Recently he considered exploring the possibility of flipping houses in the North Hills. With some of the highest home prices in the region, opportunities seem ripe for the picking. This may be true, yet the dynamic is not the same. The average homebuyer is not an urban professional, rather young families looking to raise children in a good school district. The number of bedrooms and baths drive buying decisions far more than the latest countertop material or flashy shower enclosure.

The desire to be within the best school district is so strong, I contend that any house with four bedrooms, heat and running water will sell regardless of style. And, most people in the suburbs want to blend in, not stand out. So a house built to look like the neighbor's house is more appealing than one that calls attention to itself. Conformity, becoming one of a community is at the center of the human condition.

In fact, studies have found that trees have a greater impact on house values than the style of house itself. A street lined with mature green canopies sheltering sidewalks in shade has the feel of an established community, a safer bet in selecting a home. Realtors are aware of this, despite developers who still haven't figured this out. With their propensity to clear lots for ease of construction, new developments have that new car smell, void of a history, a well lived home narrative.

I guess that's what keeps my industry in business - a year or two into one of these new homes and the buying decisions that overlooked such characteristics, soon find the cookie cutter house more of a burden than a comfort. Fitting in doesn't account for our differences, our personal preferences, our individual habits. During an open house walk through, we are sold on how we could live in a house, forgetting about how we actually live daily. Often it takes time living in a house, to flush out such things.

My own house is a good example. When we built it a dozen years ago, a studio space was taken out as the cost for construction ran over budget. It seemed like the right decision at the time. But hindsight, as it always does, has made clear it was something that has been missing from day one. A space that was needed for our household, more than some of the other rooms we kept in.

So, I have turned it over to our two boys, to design an addition they will help me build and eventually use. And as the hurricane season is upon us, I find myself in a scramble to frame it up and close it in. Providing my wife with an indoor winter project, covering the floor with her talent for mosaic tiles. But for now at the moment, the only construction going on is with the paper model designs our sons are building.

Of course, as kids usually do, the ideas they have come up with are not what one would typically find in a suburban community. Conforming is a rite of passage, something best left to adults. We moved to our neighborhood like most parents, to have our children attend a good school. On the other hand, our house does not exactly fit in. Because in creating our house, I tried to preserve some of that hurricane energy found swirling around in children. If that comes through in the new studio addition, what better place for them to exercise their creative minds?

Oct 01, 2016 02:06PM, Published by North Hills Monthly Magazine, Categories: Home+Garden, Today
http://www.northhillsmonthly.com/2016/10/01/123183/the-spiraling-housing-market

614

What is the Nature of a Home?

The house I grew up in, began as a modest sized house - three bedrooms with a single bathroom. Growing up with three sisters, my dad quickly realized a second bath was needed. And, a few interior walls shifted around over time, to squeeze in a fourth bedroom. Beyond that, things sufficed until the end of high school, when a sunroom was added to the back of our house, a place to sit with more natural light than the draped living room provided.

The latest addition to the house was a ramp I built in a day earlier this summer, to prepare for the return of my mother, after leaving for the hospital from a fall in which she could no longer get up. Until that point, my father managed to care for her daily, but that changed, so she spent many months in an assisted living facility, my father by her side.

There was a desire to bring her back home and so transformations were made in preparation. The house reminded me of a story she read when I was growing up - The Giving Tree. The selflessness of that tree always struck me, giving every part of itself, limb by limb, for another in need. I like to think our house has the same intent, giving of itself through all the changes experienced as our family grew. Now supporting my mother one last time, in her need to return home.

I have another theory about trees. In the dozen years or so that I have been living surrounded by them in my current house, I have noticed a peculiar thing. As the storms of spring and fall knock aging trees over, nearby trees catch them, holding them up, keeping them from falling completely. Some may say it is merely the result of a forest density that prevents the majority of trees from reaching the ground. But, what if there is more to it than just that?

In the life of a tree, lasting decades if not centuries, time is divided in two equal parts - growing then dying. Most trees found growing around a house never make it to the dying years. Cut down just past their prime, for fear of falling on the house as they wither away, tips of branches no longer sprouting leaves. It makes me wonder if the house is just trying to fulfill a role, a supportive forest nowhere in sight. Nevertheless, a tree can live on for many years after it has fallen in a forest, even uprooted trunks will still carry sap nurturing branches, as they reorient to the light in their new found position.

Isn't a house really a forest of trees? A thicket of wood studs standing together to form walls, roof rafters overhead a sheltering canopy. Cut down and milled, the trees of a forest become a man-made forest, transitioning into a second life as a house. Despite encasement between drywall and exterior sheathing, hidden from sight, out of mind, soon forgotten - is this the source of supportive benevolence in a house? Does the nature of a forest carry through to our home by bringing trees in to become the structure?

We seek studs out when hanging pictures on a wall. For most people, the only consideration in a 2x4 is its straightness. Walls that are flat, perfectly straight and plumb are perceived as well built. What causes a wall stud to warp or bow? There are several factors, but one relatively unknown is its orientation. Installed upside down, opposite of the direction it grew within the truck, can cause wood to bend. There was a time when carpenters were aware of such things, taking care in the handling of materials to work with their inherent flow.

However, today we live in an era of do-it-yourself lumber yards, pre-cut studs at $3 apiece, unaware of the forest from which they came. Time honored wisdom passed down through generations of craftsmen is lost on our mass produced society. This is not to say that we should return to an earlier way of life, things change and that is the natural cycle. But, to race ahead blindly, not reflecting on what we are leaving behind, is also fool hearted.

For me, the wood that goes into a house, even the pine framing that does not take center stage as hardwood flooring or a dining room table, is more than raw material. The physical properties of strength and stability are not independent of the selfless metaphysical qualities. They go hand in hand and maybe when we use trees to build a house for shelter from the elements, our homes also become infused with a supportiveness, the characteristics we feel when returning home. If we pause to notice.

Nov 01, 2016 07:14AM, Published by North Hills Monthly Magazine, Categories: Home+Garden, Today, Advertisers
http://www.northhillsmonthly.com/2016/11/01/126263/what-is-the-nature-of-a-home-

Reporting From The Front

Over a dozen years ago, we cleared a spot in the forest to build our house. Despite my attempts to minimize impact on existing habitats, several species were uprooted. In particular, a well-established ant hill within the excavation that has been moving around ever since. Ants are industrious and I have witnessed them making trials stretching several hundred yards, foraging supplies for their colonies. Needless to say, they are quite formidable foes, with annual assaults on our house that has invaded their wooded domain, the framing is an irresistible food source.

Robins, jays, sparrows and a few turtle doves were also forced to relocate from the trees we took down. Some have since taken to building nests on the dozen beams that outcrop under the roof overhangs. I let them be, since we enjoy watching from our bathroom window the young ones feed in the mornings. And, I figure we owe them something for us moving in, outsiders that disrupted their natural habitat in trees.

However, other keepers of the forest, the squirrels and field mice who gather nuts and seeds into stockpiles for winter, are not so welcome. Don't let anyone tell you the forest is an idyllic tranquil place filled with singing birds and magical sprites dancing around. Birds spend more time sounding warning calls than flirtatious melodies, since there is always something stirring, creating mischief in the woods day or night. Squirrels and field mice are relentless this time of year, climbing all over the house, scratching and gnawing away, seeking a warm wall cavity as cold temperatures are looming.

And, not to forget the trees we cut down to make room for a house. I tried to find a spot with the fewest amount and the youngest, to preserve the grander ones. Nevertheless, some were sacrificed for our benefit, red maples, sassafras, wild cherries and in hindsight, I realize now that our house sits on the site of a former pioneering tree, maybe a big tooth aspen or white pine. The natural clearing in the forest density, which was filling in with young saplings seizing access to the sky, speaks to a once large canopy that had fallen years before our arrival. Our home now stands in its place.

When I sought out a wooded site to build a home, thinking it would make a wonderful place for our kids to explore, I did not anticipate the lessons it would teach me as well. Our earliest ancestors came down out of the trees to live in grasslands a long time ago. A new frontier to inhabit, with new discoveries to be made, but what knowledge of the forest has been forgotten since we left? What will we learn if we return?

Today we find ourselves living on a planet undergoing great change and while we debate the reasons why, Mother Nature blazes ahead to correct our behavior. We may be one of the most intelligent and adaptable creatures on earth, but we are also one of the most naive and ignorant. In my profession, the architectural community preaches buildings made of locally sourced materials, with low carbon footprints and low energy consumption. However, I believe they are overlooking something of grave importance.

The trees of a forest depend on a symbiotic relationship with mycorrhizal fungi at their roots. In their exchange of glucose and sucrose for water and minerals, both the trees and fungi receive the nutrients they need to survive, while contributing to a diverse soil chemistry in a sustainable manner. A similar thing occurs within our own digestive system working with intestinal bacteria to ease absorption of nutrients from the food we eat. What if a house could be designed on this model, working with the natural environment, rather than simply reacting to it?

A small example is my own house that was built with exposed rafter tails protruding out from the walls under eaves. In the tight corner recesses, they provide the perfect dark spot for roosting bats. We see them dart around in the evenings, feasting on pesky insects. In exchange for safe harbor on our house, they provide us with a natural bug repellant, keeping mosquitoes at bay. So, we can enjoy the expanse of a star filled sky, on an open deck without need for the typical screened porch or an arsenal of chemical sprays and electric zappers. A reduction in energy and material consumption, simply by letting a fellow inhabitant of the woods do their thing.

One of my favorite Taoist sayings is to *do nothing, yet nothing is left undone (wu wei, erh wu pu wei)*. Modern medicine is founded on a similar principle - *first, do no harm*. Over time, this wisdom has been largely lost. We have become accustom to doing without thought of our actions, then remedies on top of remedies to clean up the aftermath. There seems to be a lot of wasted time and energy with this way of life.

This past summer, I attended the Venice Biennale, an exhibition of work from some of the most talented minds in the field of architecture, tackling some of the most pressing social, political, economic, environmental issues facing our world. The theme for the exhibition was an image of Maria Reiche, a German archeologist, standing atop a ladder to gain a new perspective of the landscape, departing from the usual viewpoint on the ground. What resonated with me, was the use of a simple common device, to overcome big obstacles. It is this approach, a resourcefulness with minimal means, but if also done in a symbiotic way, I believe will result in novel solutions, more attuned to the context in which we exist. A way out of our avarice and oppression.

I started this year off by calling attention to a house that was just breaking ground, an example of the typical suburban house, first clearing and then leveling the land of all natural contour and cover. I would like to end this year by checking back in with that house, reporting from the front on what has been learned, what progress has been made.

A forest desolated, for a homeowner comforted more by grasslands. Missed opportunities, much that is tragic and banal. Conventional materials of traditional methods, little sign of creativity and yet, some hope in a priority for the practical, the frugal, the here and now. Mother Nature speaks the same language, maybe we will hear.

Dec 01, 2016 08:38AM, Published by North Hills Monthly Magazine, Categories: Home+Garden, Today
http://www.northhillsmonthly.com/2016/12/01/129052/reporting-from-the-front